D1250120

Contents

89¢

The Puppet Ministry

The Puppet Ministry

with instructions and scripts

by

Jim Christy

Beacon Hill Press of Kansas City
Kansas City, Missouri

Preface

Puppets are fun—fun to see, fun to use, fun to have around.

Puppets are teaching tools. They help teach songs, Bible verses and lessons, stories and truths.

Puppets are for children. Especially young children.

Puppets are work. As with any effective method, the key to successful use is work.

Puppets are not *the* answer. They are *an* answer.

The purpose of this book is twofold:

1. To give basic principles of one kind of puppetry.

2. To provide scripts for church puppet shows based on five specific characters. (One can be invisible.) Many scripts can be used for older children (entire script). For younger children it would be better to use only the marked portion of script. Generally, the target age is 4 to 9 years.

Puppets can be used simply and without much bother. But the more refinements which are added the more effective they will be. So why not give it your best?

—JIM CHRISTY

Part One

Getting into Puppetry

The word is out. Puppets are in—in boxes, in closets, in drawers, in classrooms, in playrooms, in the way.

"Puppets" is a magic word. Children will learn from them. Children will sit quietly watching puppets. Puppets will solve discipline problems. Puppets will do great things for a sagging children's program.

Right? Right!

Except! Except?

Puppets are not human. Nor are they automatic. They are, in fact, dummies. Dumb dummies. Without a brain behind them, they are almost worthless. They just stare at everyone who wants to look at them. But in the hands of a skillful manipulator, they come alive.

So what does it take to be a "puppeteer"? It takes more than the mechanics. To know how to run a puppet, important though that is, does not make one qualified for puppet ministry. Three things are needed before anyone moves into this field:

1. A desire to work with children. Do you see the importance of investing yourself in children?

9

2. A willingness to give, say, two hours every week just for puppets.

3. A long-term commitment to the puppet ministry. *Years*, not months or a year. Years and years.

Go first class. The puppet ministry is important. Got that? Set high goals for what you will eventually have—the best puppets (have you ever had an eye fall off a puppet just before they are to go on stage? Disaster!), the best staging, the best sound, the best puppeteers, the best presentations, the best scripts.

Now at the beginning you may not have all that. But in your heart and in your plans, they are there all the time. You know. Sometime. Every addition puts you closer to your goal.

Go ahead. Dream a little. Puppets and puppet ministries are basically imaginative anyway! This book is the product of the author's own dreams . . . dreams two years old plus 400 hours of work.

You still want to get into the puppet ministry?

Let's go!

A Philosophy of Puppet Ministry

Puppets are part of a total ministry to children. They cannot be the whole program. One 5- or 10-minute presentation by puppets every week is better than entire services by puppets periodically.

Do not judge the success of your puppets by the volume of response from the children. To them, puppets are serious. Fun, but serious fun. They will laugh at the action but rarely the message. Entertainment is a goal but certainly not primary. Here are the basic objectives of a puppet ministry:

1. To teach

a. To teach the children
  (1) About Jesus, what He did and what He will do for them
  (2) About the Bible, its message for them today
  (3) About the church, their church

b. To teach teens—the puppeteers themselves
  (1) The truths they are teaching the children through puppets. As they teach, they learn.
  (2) How to teach and share their faith in Christ
  (3) To be faithful in a ministry to others
  (4) To work with one another
  (5) Skills for future ministry

2. To win children and teens to Christ and the church

3. To establish in the faith

a. To establish children
  (1) In the joy of serving Christ
  (2) In faithfulness to the church

b. To establish teens
  (1) In their spiritual lives
  (2) In their commitment to each other and hence the church
  (3) In self-confidence as individuals

What obviously has evolved is a twofold objective: development of both the children and the teens. In fact, we have discovered more noticeable growth among the teen puppeteers than we have the children.

Long-range objectives like these do not demand results in two or three weeks. (A four-year-old could conceiveably be involved in this ministry for 15 years. First as a hearer, then as a doer.) Time is part of the process.

11

A puppet takes on a personality to a small child, and he identifies with it. It becomes his friend. It comes to church just like he does. It has the same needs and problems and joys he has. As it deals with certain situations, it helps the child deal with his. The puppet is not a big person looking down at the child. It is a child living in a child's world with big folk around.

Therefore a puppet needs to have a constant personality. It cannot be Joe this week, Paul last week, and Butch next week. Last week's Jane the Goof-off can't become this week's Ruth the Saint. It must be the same, week after week after week. His name and his voice should be unchanged also.

His world must not change, either, unless it is clearly explained and accounted for by the puppets themselves. If a puppet is replaced, the replacement should be carefully explained. (We replaced one puppet, and nine months later a child asked how "Geronimo" was doing.)

Because objectives are long-range, no one script should attempt to give the children everything at once. A little each week will get the truths across better than everything in one presentation. Aim to get one key point across with each presentation.

How to Get Started

1. *Spend some money.* For a starter, order four people puppets. Everyone knows someone who makes puppets. Run from them. A puppet will be used as much as 200 hours a year by not-too-careful teens. We tried making our own. Then we tried the put-it-together-yourself kit. They simply cannot compare with those produced by expert puppet makers. Besides, we ended up spending more than it looked like at first for our bargains.

We have used both rod-controlled arms and gloved hands of puppeteers. We think the gloved hand puppets are more effective and allow a beginning puppeteer an opportunity to get in on the action.

2. *Begin recruiting teens to assist.* Set simple rules and enforce them. We have three rules:

    a. You must be at all practices and performances unless advance arrangements are made.

    b. You must follow any rules set down by the group. (Recently our puppeteers asked that anyone late for practice be required to sit out the next presentation.)

    c. You commit yourself to this ministry until June 1. In June new commitments are made.

3. When the puppets arrive, *get used to them yourself.* Then introduce them to your puppeteers. Most puppet producers provide "How To" manuals for their puppets.

4. *Develop technique.* Assume it will take 20 hours of practice per puppeteer before any presentations are given.

5. Secure a foot-locker trunk (or large suitcase) with a lock on it. Always keep the puppets in the trunk. Stubbornly insist that no one but the puppeteers see the puppets "off stage." This serves a twofold purpose:

    a. It builds a sense of privilege for the puppeteers. Not everyone gets to handle the puppets.

    b. It protects the image a young child has of the puppet. He only sees it animated, never flopped over as though dead.

6. *Build a stage.* We tried pianos, boards, and all sorts of makeshift things. We did not like them. There were too many problems to be solved every time. We have three

kinds of stages. The one we like best is the simplest and the biggest one. Here is a diagram of it:

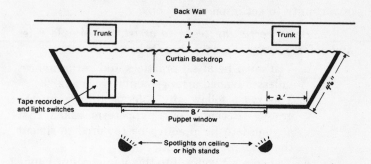

Curtain may be attached to the ceiling or hung from a bar or wire. If necessary, the wall itself could be used as the backdrop, eliminating the curtain. Be sure to allow sufficient room for puppeteers to move around behind the stage. They are *never* allowed to stand up in front of the curtain.

Here is a front view:

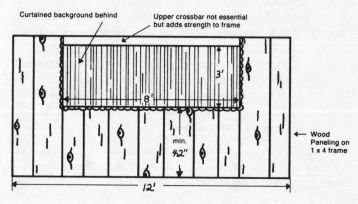

14

Here is a view of the back side:

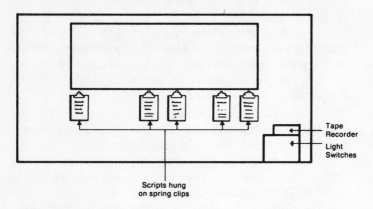

Scripts hung
on spring clips

A permanently installed stage is ideal, but it can be made portable. The curtain can be hung on plastic plumber's pipe. A small-window stage can be used for one or two puppets.

7. *Secure a tape recorder.* A small cassette player is good to begin with, but if you are serious about puppets and use them often, you will sense the need for a better sound system.

8. *Get scripts.* That is the tough job. Most scripts are irrelevant to your needs or are written by adults for adults, with perhaps some children terms tossed in. Besides, you will need a new script nearly every week. This book has about a four months' supply. Make six copies of all scripts, record them on tape, file the copies by name with the location on the tape listed by number. At first this seems unimportant, but when you have 100 or 200 scripts on tape and in files, a system becomes imperative to be able to get to them for future use.

We rarely do live performances. Mikes, sound effects, and misreading of scripts involve too much risk. Besides, it allows us to use the teens whose reading and impersonation abilities are the best for this work and let others do the manipulating.

Record scripts on tape, using the same voices for each character each week. The voices can be puppeteers, adults, or any good readers who will be at every recording session. We use the puppeteers. They get comfortable with the script before it is presented.

9. *Practice from the tape.* Practice and practice and practice. Keep puppeteers on the same puppet or puppet's hands at all times. Do not change parts, etc.

Do not worry too much about the puppeteers "goofing off" some at practice. They have an uncanny ability to know when things need to get serious.

Go through the script with the tape at least three times. If possible, go through a rehearsal just before actual presentation.

10. *Present the program.* It is a long way from 1 to 10. When the puppets arrive, there is an intense pressure to try them out on the children immediately. For the sake of a long-range ministry, be sure you are ready before you begin. The puppeteers will respond to something well done. Do not yield to the temptation to show off the puppets prematurely.

Practice Schedule

1. Set a practice time and let puppeteers know well in advance so there will be no excuses.

2. Have a recorder set up and ready to go.

3. At practice, give each puppeteer a copy of the script. (Do not send copies home with them.)

4. Have them read it to themselves.

5. Rehearse the script (As many times as needed).

6. Record the script. Note number location on tape.

7. Get the puppets out.

8. Clip the scripts up where the puppeteers can follow them.

9. Practice the puppets with the tape. Remember, most puppeteers do better during the presentation than the practice.

10. If possible, go through it once just before presentation.

Part Two

Performance Scripts

About These Scripts
- All these scripts have the same five characters.
- If you record them yourselves, the names can be changed.
- If you have only four puppets, or no lion, Leo can be invisible.
- Scripts can be used as they are or if a shorter version is desired, start from the asterisk.

Personality Sketches of the Five Puppets

Leo the Lion. He is the authority. His growl and voice speak with assurance. The idea comes from C. S. Lewis's *Chronicles of Narnia* lion. He is the favorite of the children, though they are a bit afraid of his loud growl.

Lucy. She is a girl who talks a great deal. She carries flowers, messes with her hair, and has a lot of pride. She and Harvey fight all of the time. She has a clever mind.

Harvey. He is a boy with a quick mind, plenty of nerve, and too much mischief. He is always creating havoc and pointing out others' weaknesses. Usually he gets caught. Underneath it all, he is very spiritual and generous.

Christopher. He is a boy who is intellectual, sophisticated, and generally bored with the ordinary. He rarely is in conflict with anyone and is extremely self-confident.

Whitzit. He is a boy, not too bright, tries to mimic the others, usually goofs, is mechanically inclined, and is the only one who can fix things.

✳ ✳ ✳

David Meets Goliath

SCRIPTURE: 1 Samuel 17
CONCEPT: God helps us to do things for Him.

WHITZIT: Boys and girls, today we will be telling you the story of a boy who let God use him. *(Exit)*

CHRISTOPHER: Boys and girls, today we will be telling you about a man who thought he could do anything he wanted without God's help. *(Exit)*

LUCY: Boys and girls, in just a couple of minutes we will tell you about some big soldiers who were afraid and would not let God help them. *(Exit)*

HARVEY: Hi gang! You are about to hear how rocks were better than sticks and steel, because God was helping the rock carrier. *(Exit)*

LEO: And now . . . the story of David the Shepherd Boy and Goliath the Giant. *(Exit) (Lucy appears at side.)*

LUCY: The soldiers of King Saul were fighting the soldiers of Giant Goliath. Every day both armies would get together on the hills ready to fight. Goliath would yell out . . .

19

WHITZIT *(with hat on):* Is there anyone there who is not afraid to come over and fight me? Why, I'll tear him to pieces and feed him to the birds. Ha. Ha. Ha.

LUCY: This frightened the soldiers of King Saul.

CHRISTOPHER: Is there anyone who will go fight the giant? *(On tape—not me; or me; oh, no, I won't.)* What am I going to do? Search around and see if anyone will.

LUCY: They searched and found no one. Meanwhile, David had been sent by his father with food for the army. *(He goes across stage both ways as if walking, carrying a knapsack.)* He comes to the army just as Goliath yells . . .

WHITZIT: Is there anyone there who is not afraid to come over and fight me? I'll tear him to pieces and feed him to the birds. Ha. Ha. Ha.

HARVEY: O King Saul, who is going to go fight that giant?

CHRISTOPHER: I cannot find anyone who is not afraid.

WHITZIT: Let's see if your God can deliver you from me. Ha. Ha. Ha. Is He gone? Is your God asleep?

HARVEY: O King, that giant is making fun of God.

CHRISTOPHER: I know. I know.

HARVEY: Are you going to let him get by with that?

CHRISTOPHER: What can I do?

HARVEY: Go fight him. God will take care of you.

CHRISTOPHER: Who, me?

WHITZIT: Where is your great God?

HARVEY: I won't let him get away with that. I'll go fight the giant!

CHRISTOPHER: You?

HARVEY: Yes, me.

CHRISTOPHER: Are you sure?

HARVEY: God helped me once when I killed a bear trying to steal a lamb. Another time He gave me strength to kill a lion.

CHRISTOPHER: If you go fight Goliath you will need some armor. Put these on. *(Harvey exits.)* I don't know if I should let a young man like that go. Goliath is strong and brave. *(Harvey returns.)*

HARVEY: King Saul, I cannot wear your armor. It is too heavy and big. I will fight Goliath without it.

CHRISTOPHER: Here, take my sword.

HARVEY: No. I wouldn't know how to use it. I know how to use my slingshot better than that.

CHRISTOPHER: OK. I hope you are safe. *(Harvey and Christopher exit.)*

LUCY: David got ready to fight the giant. He went to the stream where he picked up five smooth stones. He then began moving toward Goliath.

WHITZIT: What? You send a child to fight me? Why, I'll tear him to pieces. Then I'll destroy your army.

HARVEY: Goliath, you made fun of God. God is not gone. He is not asleep. He is with me and I'm going to prove it.

LUCY: David ran toward Goliath, put a stone in his sling and flung it as hard as he could. And Goliath fell down dead.

HARVEY: God helped me do it. Thank You, God. *(All exit as Leo comes in.)*

LEO: Boys and girls, never be afraid to do what God wants you to do. No matter how hard it looks, you can do it with God's help. Remember, David trusted God and conquered the giant. You can trust God and He will help you. So long. *(Growl.)*

Paul and Silas in Jail

SCRIPTURE: Acts 16:23-34

CONCEPT: God uses hard places for good if we trust Him.

LEO: Hello. I'm Leo the Lion. Today I have good news for you. My friends—Harvey, Whitzit, Christopher, and Lucy—are going to help me. We are going to tell you about two men who trusted God when they were in trouble and God helped them. If you do your best, God will help you, too, when you are in trouble. Harvey! *(Harvey appears.)*

HARVEY: Yes, Leo?

LEO: Harvey, will you be Paul this morning? We are going to tell everyone here about Paul's troubles.

HARVEY: Sure, Leo.

LEO: Christopher! *(Christopher appears.)*

CHRISTOPHER: Did you call me, Leo?

LEO: Yes, I did, Christopher. I want you to help me tell a story. Will you be Silas?

CHRISTOPHER: I'll be glad to.

LEO: Whitzit! *(Whitzit appears.)*

WHITZIT: Good morning, everyone.

LEO: Whitzit, I want you to help us tell the story of Paul and Silas in jail. Will you be the jailer?

WHITZIT: I will.

LEO: Lucy! Lucy! *(Lucy appears.)*

LUCY: My, my, what a lovely day. I have my hair all combed, my dress ironed, my . . .

LEO: Lucy, will you help us tell the story of Paul and Silas in jail? Will you be the jailer's other prisoner?

LUCY: I will be happy to do that if you think this dress will be alright. It is a little . . .

LEO: That will be fine, Lucy. Shall we begin? *(All exit except Leo.)*

* One day Paul and Silas arrived in the town of Philippi. *(Harvey and Christopher appear as if walking together.)*

HARVEY: Silas, this looks like a friendly town. The people will want to hear about Jesus, I am sure.

CHRISTOPHER: I am not sure, Paul. Some of the people look mean.

HARVEY: We will have to find out. Let's go into town and find a place to preach. *(Both exit.)*

LEO: Paul and Silas did not find a church to preach in. They did find some ladies having church outside, down by the river, and preached to them. Each week they did this and more and more people came to hear them. *(Harvey and Christopher appear.)*

HARVEY: Silas, isn't it wonderdul to know all these people love Jesus like we do?

CHRISTOPHER: It is, Paul. I was not sure anyone would want to hear about Jesus. I was wrong. Lots of people are happy to know about Him.

HARVEY: Look at all those people over there. Are they coming over here? Do you think they want to hear us preach?

CHRISTOPHER: Paul, I think they are coming over here to see us. I am not sure they want to hear us preach. They look angry.

HARVEY: Yes, they do look angry. Let's see what they want.

WHITZIT: Are you Paul of Tarsus and Silas of Antioch?

HARVEY: Yes, we are. What can we do for you?

23

WHITZIT: I am the jailer. You are under arrest. Come to the jail with me.

CHRISTOPHER: Could you tell us why you are arresting us?

WHITZIT: You have been causing riots in town. That is against the law. Come along with me. *(All three exit.)*

LEO: Paul and Silas were taken by the jailer to prison. First he made them take their shirts off. Then he had both of them beaten on the back until their backs were red with blood. After that, the two men were placed in a dungeon—that's a small prison cell underground.

HARVEY: Silas, is your back hurting pretty bad?

CHRISTOPHER: Oh, I have never hurt so much before in my life. Oh . . .

HARVEY: I know how much it hurts. But I keep thinking God can help us.

CHRISTOPHER: I hope so. We really need His help.

HARVEY: Why don't we ask God to help us? Both of us can pray.

CHRISTOPHER: Let's do. Before we do, though, will you sing a song to cheer me up a little and help me forget about my back?

HARVEY: *(Singing) There is nothing can compare*
With the fellowship we share,
God and His children.
For their lives are satisfied
As they're walking side by side,
God with His children.
Not in pleasant paths alone are
ways made bright;
Peace comes from God while
walking in His light;
Peace comes from God while
walking in His light.†

CHRISTOPHER: I feel much better now. God is with us. I know He is taking care of us, too. I am not afraid.

HARVEY: Nor am I.

LEO: Paul and Silas prayed and sang together. Nearby were other prisoners who listened to them. *(Harvey and Christopher cover their eyes as if praying. Lucy appears and watches.)*

As they were praying and singing, suddenly an earthquake shook the jail. All the doors broke open and all the prisoners were freed from their chains. *(All three exit.)*

WHITZIT: Oh, no! All the prisoners have escaped. I will get killed for this. I might as well kill myself now.

HARVEY: *(Appearing.)* Jailer! Jailer!

WHITZIT: Do I hear someone?

HARVEY: Jailer! It is I, Paul of Tarsus. Do not kill yourself. We are all safe. No one has escaped. Everyone is still here.

WHITZIT: O Paul. Thank you. Thank you. You were singing about Jesus and praying to Him. Tell me and my family what we must do to be saved.

HARVEY: I will be glad to tell you. Let's go talk about it now. *(They exit.)*

LEO: Paul told the jailer and his family about Jesus and they all became Christians. God used Paul and Silas in jail even though being beaten and locked up were not good things to have happen to them. And boys and girls, God can use you even when bad things happen to you. Remember that! *(Growl.)*

The Calling of Samuel

SCRIPTURE: 1 Samuel 3

CONCEPT: When God calls us to follow Him, He wants to help us.

LUCY: Oh, I'm sleepy this morning. I hardly slept a wink.

CHRISTOPHER: Why, Lucy? Were you sick?

LUCY: No. I was hearing all kinds of voices. I was a little afraid.

CHRISTOPHER: That's funny. I didn't hear a thing.

LUCY: I'm surprised your snoring didn't wake you up. You snore like a train.

CHRISTOPHER: At least I sleep. (Whitzit enters.)

WHITZIT: Boy, am I sleepy this morning. I didn't sleep very good at all. Say, Christopher, has anyone told you how loud you snore? You sound like a train. Like this. (Snores)

CHRISTOPHER: I don't snore like that.

WHITZIT: You do, too.

CHRISTOPHER: I do not.

WHITZIT: You do, too.

LUCY: See, Christopher, I told you.

CHRISTOPHER: OK! OK! But that's not what kept you two awake.

LUCY: I wonder what did. (Harvey enters.)

HARVEY: Oh, I'm sleepy. I didn't sleep a wink last night. Christopher, old buddy, did you know you snore loud? It sounds like a . . .

CHRISTOPHER: I know! I know! A train.

HARVEY: How did you know?

CHRISTOPHER: Lucy and Whitzit could not sleep either. They told me.

HARVEY: Why couldn't you sleep?

LUCY: We don't know, Harvey.

HARVEY: Do you think Leo might know? *(Leo appears.)* Hi, Leo. We wanted to ask you a question. Lucy and Whitzit and I did not sleep very well last night. Do you know why?

LEO: Yes, I think I know why.

LUCY: Tell us, Leo.

WHITZIT: Yes, we want to know.

LEO: When I got up this morning I found one of you had left the record player on and a record was going around and around. The noise of the needle made a funny sound.

LUCY: Of course! That's what I heard. Harvey, you are going to have to be more careful with that record player.

HARVEY: Me! I didn't do it.

LUCY: Then it must have been you, Whitzit.

WHITZIT: No, I didn't use the record player last night.

LUCY: Christopher, why aren't you more careful?

CHRISTOPHER: No, I didn't do it.

LEO: Lucy? Did you use the record player last night?

LUCY: Uh . . . uh . . .

LEO: Lucy . . . did you?

LUCY: Yes, I did. I'm the one, I guess. I forgot I had listened to a record.

WHITZIT: And that snoring sound wasn't Christopher was it?

HARVEY: No. It was the record player.

CHRISTOPHER: That's good to know.

LEO: Night sounds can sound scary.

27

HARVEY: They sure can. *(Pause)* I was wondering how Samuel must have felt the night God called him. I would have been scared.

LEO: Yes . . . that's right. God did call Samuel in the night.

LUCY: I don't remember that story, will you tell it to us?

LEO: Sure. Let's take turns. I'll begin.

* One day the priest Eli heard a woman praying to God. She asked God to give her a son. She had no children and wanted at least one. Eli stopped the woman and told her God had heard her prayer. She would have a son.

CHRISTOPHER: And she and her husband did have a son. They named him Samuel. As soon as he was old enough to take care of himself, his parents brought him to Eli to help take care of the House of God. They were glad God answered their prayer.

WHITZIT: Samuel lived with Eli. He helped Eli. He kept the House of the Lord clean. He opened and closed the doors. He helped visitors. He did all he could to help Eli. Every year his mother and father came to see him and brought him new clothes to wear.

HARVEY: Samuel slept in the House of the Lord. So did Eli. One night Samuel and Eli were in bed when Samuel heard someone call his name, "Samuel, Samuel." He jumped out of bed and ran to Eli. "What do you want?" he asked. Eli said, "I did not call you, go back to bed." Samuel went back to his room and got in bed.

LEO: Samuel was just about asleep when he heard his name again, "Samuel, Samuel." Again he jumped out of bed and ran to Eli. "What do you want?" he asked. Eli rubbed his eyes and said, "Samuel, I didn't call you. Go back to bed."

28

CHRISTOPHER: Samuel went back to bed again wondering what was happening. He was sure he had heard his name. And, sure enough, he heard it again, "Samuel, Samuel." Again he jumped out of bed and ran to Eli. No one else was in the house. "Eli," he said, "you called me, what do you want?"

WHITZIT: Eli realized by now that God was calling Samuel. He said to him, "My child, you hear the voice of God calling to you. The next time you hear your name, say, 'Speak, my Lord, your servant is listening.'" Samuel went back to bed.

HARVEY: Now Samuel could not sleep. What was it like to have God talk to you? Was God mean or kind? Then he heard his name again. "Samuel, Samuel." This time Samuel said, "Speak, my Lord, for your servant is listening." God then told Samuel He wanted Samuel to love and serve Him all his life. Samuel said he would.

LEO: When God talks to us, He is kind and loving and always wants to help us.

LUCY: I liked that story. Thanks for telling it.

LEO: Good-by everyone. *(Growl.)*

✳ ✳ ✳

Fiery Furnace Story

SCRIPTURE: Daniel 3

CONCEPT: God takes care of those who trust and obey Him.

LEO: It sure is quiet today. I wonder where everyone is? No one was downstairs. Lucy? Christopher? Harvey? Whitzit? No answer. *(Background—the sound of a trumpet, etc.)* Oh, no! I forgot. I forgot. Today is the big parade. I better hurry or I will be late. Good-by, everyone. *(Exits) (Harvey, Christopher, Lucy, and Whitzit enter, watch parade go by, music of band and parade sounds.)*

HARVEY: *(Humming to sound of music. Others join him in a kind of celebration.)*

WHITZIT: Look! Look! A clown!

LUCY: Oh, I wish I could have a balloon. I always have wanted one. It's more fun to have one.

HARVEY: I love to pop 'em. Bang. Bang. Bang.

LUCY: Not *my* balloon!

CHRISTOPHER: I would rather have a cotton candy myself. A pink, big one. It is really fun to eat.

WHITZIT: Where's Leo?

LUCY: Oh, no! I forgot to wake him up. He's still sleeping.

CHRISTOPHER: And he just loves parades.

HARVEY: What shall we do?

LUCY: Look! Here comes some more of the parade.

WHITZIT: It's another band.

HARVEY: But look who's leading the band. It's Leo! Leo is directing the band with his tail. That's good. Yea, Leo! Come on everyone, cheer!

ALL: Yea, Leo! Yea! Yea! Yea!

LUCY: We better get home. The parade is over. *(All exit. All appear again except Leo.)*

HARVEY: That was a great parade. I liked it. The clowns, the bands, the floats, and the horses.

LUCY: I liked Leo the best. Did you see how he moved his tail to direct the band?

CHRISTOPHER: I wonder who woke him up?

WHITZIT: I don't know, but I'm sure glad he woke up. He was the star of the parade.

LEO: *(Enters carrying four balloons.)* Hello, Lucy. Hello, Whitzit. Hello, Harvey. Hello, Christopher. I brought everyone a balloon.

HARVEY: Thank you, Leo. Can I have the red one?

WHITZIT: And I'll take the yellow one.

CHRISTOPHER: I would like the blue one.

LUCY: It doesn't matter what color I get. Thank you, Leo.

LEO: You are welcome, everyone.

LUCY: Leo, I had a question to ask you.

LEO: What is it, Lucy?

LUCY: Were there any parades told about in the Bible?

LEO: Let's see . . . uh . . . uh.

CHRISTOPHER: I know of a parade that was bad and turned out good.

WHITZIT: Huh?

CHRISTOPHER: The Bible tells about a parade that was bad but that turned out good.

LUCY: Tell us about it, Christopher.

CHRISTOPHER: It all began when a king decided he wanted everyone to celebrate his birthday with a big parade. He would go along and everyone would bow down to him as he went by.

HARVEY: That was Nebuca-something, wasn't it?

CHRISTOPHER: Leo, can you remember the king's name?

LEO: It was Nebuchadnezzar. Let's act out the story, OK?

WHITZIT: Good. *(All exit.) (Harvey returns with a crown on.)*

*HARVEY: I'm Nebuchadnezzar, the greatest king in all the world. No one greater than I has ever lived. I am making a new law. Everyone must bow down and worship me and my idol. Me! Me! Do you hear that? Everyone! Anyone who does not bow down will be

31

thrown into the furnace and be burned to a crisp. Bow down to me and my idol when I come by. *(Lucy, Whitzit and Christopher appear and whisper together.)*

LUCY: Oh, Meshach, what are we going to do? We serve the living God. We cannot bow down and worship a man, even if he is a king.

WHITZIT: What shall we do?

CHRISTOPHER: Why, Shadrach and Meshach, we shall not bow down to that king. I would rather die than do that. No! We serve only the living God. *(All exit.)*

HARVEY: Here I am. Here I am. Everyone bow down. I am great, I am good. I am God! Bow down. Everyone bow down . . . hey, you three . . . down there. Didn't you hear? Bow down. Bow down before me, Nebuchadnezzar, the great, marvelous king.

CHRISTOPHER: *(From offstage.)* O King Nebuchadnezzar, we will do no such thing. We serve the true and living God. We bow down to Him. But not to you. No! We will not do it.

HARVEY: Is that right? What about you other two? Speak for yourselves. Don't let him speak for you. Are you going to bow down to me?

WHITZIT: No, O great king. We are not going to bow down to you. I will not do it.

HARVEY: And what about you?

LUCY: King Nebuchadnezzar, we respect you as our king. But you are not our god. We will not bow down to you. No! I will not either.

HARVEY: What? You mean you will not do it? Do you know what will happen to you?

CHRISTOPHER: Yes, oh king. We know. We will be thrown into the burning furnace. If the living God

32

wants to save us, He will. If not, we would rather die than bow down to you or any ugly idol you make.

HARVEY: Oh! I'm so angry I could throw you in myself! Guards! Guards! Throw these three into the fire. Let them die there. That should fix them good. Ha. Ha. Ha. No one else will dare not to bow down now. Why, I'm the greatest . . . WHAT? My eyes must be playing tricks on me. Guards! Guards! How many men did you throw into that fire? . . . you say three? That's what I thought, but I see four. The fourth one looks different. Why didn't you tie their hands and feet? . . . You did? How can they walk around then? Open the door. Tell them to come out. Oh, they must be brave men to be able to walk around in the fire like that. *(The three appear.)* How did you do it, boys?

CHRISTOPHER: O King Nebuchadnezzar, we did not do it. God delivered us out of the power of the fire. The living God did it.

LUCY: Yes, He did. He did. He saved us.

WHITZIT: He was with us in the fire, too. What a wonderful God He is!

HARVEY: Yes, yes. He *is* wonderful. I am sorry I thought I could be God. I cannot be. I can only worship Him. God is great. *(All exit, Leo enters.)*

LEO: The parade looked like trouble for Shadrach, Meshach, and Abednego. But they trusted God to help them and He did. That's just like God. Good-by, everyone. *(Growl and exit.)*

Daniel in the Lions' Den

SCRIPTURE: Daniel 6

CONCEPT: God takes care of those who trust and obey Him.

CHRISTOPHER: Hello, friends. Today I want to share you an event of unusual importance. The majority of this story concerns a princely person of unswerving allegiance to God. This event occurred about 250 centuries ago, in the cultural center of the day, Babylon.

LUCY: *(Appearing.)* Christopher. Christopher. I have to talk with you.

CHRISTOPHER: What is it, Lucy?

LUCY: Come here, Christopher. *(She whispers in his ear —pss, pss, pss, pss, Leo, pss, pss, tell, pss, pss, pss, not you!)*

CHRISTOPHER: That's not true!

LUCY: It *is*, too. I'll prove it. Harvey! Harvey! Oh, Harvey!

HARVEY: *(Appearing.)* Sisters are such a joy to have around because they make going to school easy. The quiet of the classroom is such a relief.

LUCY: Harvey, will you be quiet once! Just once . . . so *I* can talk.

HARVEY: So *you* can talk? When did you ever stop?

LUCY: Harvey! *(Fighting noise.)*

CHRISTOPHER: *(Clears throat very loud. All get quiet.)* Harvey and Lucy were trying to verify a statement she had just made. Was it Leo the lion who . . .

34

LUCY: Christopher! Don't say it! *(She whispers in Harvey's ear—pss, pss, pss, Leo, pss, pss, pss, lion, pss, pss, not Christopher.)*

HARVEY: Lucy, is that true? Leo. Leo. Leo! *(Harvey leaves.)*

LUCY: *That thing* is my brother.

CHRISTOPHER: Mine, too. *(Both exit. Harvey and Leo enter.)*

HARVEY: Leo, I want to ask you something.

LEO: Go ahead, Harvey.

HARVEY: Leo, did you ever live in Babylon?

LEO: Sure, Harvey. Why?

HARVEY: D-D-Did you ever e-e-e-eat an-an-anyone?

LEO: Of course, Harvey.

HARVEY: W-W-Well, I-I-I think I-I-I'll be g-g-going. G-G-Good-by.

LEO: Harvey. I do not eat people anymore. Let me tell you about the time I did.

HARVEY: OK, Leo. B-B-But you promise you will not eat any boys.

LEO: Nor girls. Now to my story. *(Harvey exits.)*

*   I am an Asian lion, born and raised in the great, high mountains of India. My family is the finest and most beautiful lion family in the world. Because of that, we have always been hunted for trophies and zoos. I was captured as a cub and carried to Babylon. There I was kept in a dark cage and seldom fed. In the spring of Darius's third year as king of Babylon, we were starved nearly to death. I was afraid the other lions would eat me.

One day the upper trapdoor was opened. A shaft of bright sunshine streamed down. Suddenly we saw a foot, then a leg; another foot and leg, and finally a whole body came falling into our den. We all rushed to eat. . . .

But a strange thing happened. The man fell on our backs and did not even get hurt. He stood up and our king lion jumped toward him to tear a leg off. He missed and went to the corner and laid down. Not a one of us touched the man. Finally the man came over to me, laid down, put his head on my back and went to sleep. Not one of us touched him. As he was going to sleep he sang a song. This is how it goes: *(Song) Thank You, Lord. Thank You, Lord. Thank You, Lord for what You've done.*†

WHITZIT: *(Appearing, along with Lucy and Christopher)* Leo, we've been listening to you. That is exciting!

LEO: Well, he slept all night by me. I helped keep him warm. I was so hungry I could not sleep, but I did not hurt the man. In the morning they opened the door and yelled in. The man yelled back. Then they threw a rope in and pulled him out. . . . By then we were all so hungry all we could do was growl. They opened the door again and in came some other people. This time we ate and ate. *(Lucy, Christopher, and Whitzit disappear.)* Where did they go? *(Looks around.)*

HARVEY: *(Appearing at far end of curtain.)* Leo . . . *(whispering)* . . . Leo.

LEO: Yes, Harvey?

HARVEY: *(In soft voice.)* Leo, why didn't you eat the first man?

LEO: Because God was protecting him, like He protects all His children. Oh, after telling my story I'm so

†By Otis Skillings, © 1971 by Lillenas Publishing Co. All rights reserved. Used by permission.

hungry I could eat . . . *(Looks at Harvey, reaches out his paw toward him. Harvey quickly disappears.)* . . . two all-beef patties, special sauce, lettuce, cheese, pickles, onions, on a sesame-seed bun.

So long, boys and girls. Remember, Jesus can protect you, too, when you are afraid. *(Growl.)*

* * *

The Battle of Jericho

SCRIPTURE: Joshua 5 & 6
TRUTH: God helps us do things for Him.

HARVEY: *(Singing) Joshua fit the battle of Jericho,*
                Jericho, Jericho.
                Joshua fit the battle of Jericho,
                And the walls came tumblin'
                down.
LUCY: Say, Harvey, that was good.
HARVEY: Thank you. Thank you.
LUCY: What were you singing about?
HARVEY: About the walls of Jericho falling.
LUCY: Jericho? Where's that?
HARVEY: Oh, I don't know. I don't think it is near here.
LUCY: Let's see if Christopher knows. Christopher. Christopher!
CHRISTOPHER: Lucy, I hope this is important, for I was just in the middle of the most interesting facts about . . .

LUCY: Harvey and I were wondering where Jericho is?

CHRISTOPHER: I've never heard of the place. Maybe Leo knows. I'll get him. *(Exits and returns with Leo.)*

LEO: No, I don't know where Jericho is, either. Do you think Whitzit might know?

LUCY: Whitzit? No.

HARVEY: Whitzit? No.

CHRISTOPHER: Whitzit? No.

WHITZIT: *(Enters)* Did I hear my name?

LEO: Yes, we were just wondering if you might know where Jericho is?

WHITZIT: Sure, I know.

LUCY: You do?

WHITZIT: Yes, it is in Israel. It was the most important town in the country because of its location and its water supply. Its location was important because it was near a main crossing on the Jordan River and on one of the highways to Egypt from the north and east. It was important because it had the biggest and best spring in that area, which was a desert.

CHRISTOPHER: How did you know, Whitzit?

WHITZIT: I heard Harvey singing and I wondered where it was. I read about it in a book. Say, Harvey . . .

HARVEY: Yeh, Whitzit?

WHITZIT: Will you tell us the story you were singing about?

HARVEY: OK. I like that story from the Bible. *(Pause.)* *The children of Israel had been traveling about in the desert for many years.

CHRISTOPHER: It was 40 years in all, I believe.

HARVEY: That's right. One day God talked to their leader, Joshua, and told him it was time to move into the land He had promised to them and in which

38

Abraham and their ancestors had lived. He talked with the other leaders and they agreed. They led all the people into their new land by crossing the Jordan River. God helped them cross the river.

LUCY: Is that where He stopped the water from flowing and they walked across on the bottom of the river?

HARVEY: Yes, wasn't that wonderful? Well, when they got to the new land, right ahead of them was the biggest and most important city in the area—Jericho. God told them to go take the city. He said they were to march around the city walls once a day for six days. On the seventh day they were to march around it seven times, then make a huge noise.

WHITZIT: I think that sounds silly. I don't know if I would have obeyed or not.

LEO: You are right, Whitzit. It is not always easy to do what God wants us to do. But it is important that we obey God, even if it seems silly.

HARVEY: Joshua and the children of Israel obeyed God. Each day for six days they marched around the city. On the seventh day they marched around the walls of the city seven times. Then they yelled and blew trumpets. The walls came crashing down.

LUCY: I'm sure they were glad they had obeyed God.

CHRISTOPHER: Yes. They had not only captured the largest city in the area but they could now use that beautiful spring.

LEO: They did what God wanted them to do. I hope we learn to obey God, too.

LUCY: Leo, I was thinking about that story.

LEO: What were you thinking?

LUCY: Did the children of Israel know God was going to make the walls fall down?

CHRISTOPHER: Come to think of it, they didn't. All they knew was that they were to march around the city and at the end blow their trumpets. But they did what God told them.

LEO: Yes, I believe you are right. No matter what God wants us to do, we should obey him and do it. He will help us do it. Good-by. *(Growl.)*

* * *

Jonah and the Whale

SCRIPTURE: Jonah

CONCEPT: Obeying God is the best way to live.

CHRISTOPHER: Let's see. What rhymes with porcupine? Uh . . . uh . . .
The day was da da da da
When the boy saw the porcupine.
He petted the cute little thing,
Ouch! Ouch! Ouch! Did it sting!

HARVEY: Christmas time?

CHRISTOPHER: No! Pine, not pime.

LUCY: Pine? Dine. Fine. Kine.

HARVEY: Kine?

LUCY: Yes, Harvey, dear brother, kine. K-I-N-E.

HARVEY: Kine? Be kine to me? I like that kine of sausage? Kine? K-I-N-E?

LUCY: Harvey. The word is kine. It means cows.

HARVEY: Oh, sure, I can hear the kine mooing so I better go milk the kine!

CHRISTOPHER: I do need a word. Please help me.

LUCY: I'm trying, I'm trying, Christopher, but Harvey knows so few words. Let's see. *Kine,* vine, shine.

WHITZIT: How about sunshine?

CHRISTOPHER: That's it! Listen . . .
The day was bright with sunshine
When the boy saw the porcupine.
He petted the cute little thing,
Ouch! Ouch! Ouch! Did it sting!

WHITZIT: Here's my poem . . .
There is nothing as pretty
    As a tree that is green,
If in the middle of the city
    It can be seen.

LUCY: Whitzit, that's good.

WHITZIT: Thank you. How about your poem?

LUCY: (Clears throat.)
The world is a busy place,
It shows on everybody's face.
There is little charm and grace,
When you run to win the race.

HARVEY: And now, my poem . . .
Twinkle, twinkle little star,
How I wonder what you are.
Up above the world so high,
Like a diamond in the sky.

LUCY: Harvey!

HARVEY: What?

LUCY: Harvey, you did you write that poem.

HARVEY: How'd you know?

CHRISTOPHER: We all know that poem.

HARVEY: I was just teasing. Here's my real one . . .
It's fun to be a little tease,
To tell a story with some ease.

It's fun to be a little tease,
To throw some pepper and make you sneeze.

WHITZIT: Leo, do you have a poem?

LEO: Yes, and I want all of you to help me read it. OK?

ALL: Sure. OK.

CHRISTOPHER: What's the poem about?

LEO: The poem is about Jonah. Harvey, will you be the singer? Christopher, you be Jonah; Whitzit, you be the sailor; and Lucy, you be the narrator. I'll be the voice of God. Ready? Let's begin.

HARVEY: *(Singing, making up tune as he goes.)*
*   (1) *I wonder how it felt to be snatched by a great*
        big mouth
     As Jonah was, while running away to the South.
  (2) *I wonder how it felt to be eaten in one big bite*
     By a whale with a great big appetite.
  (3) *I wonder how it felt to be swallowed by a great*
        big whale
     By a whale with a great big tail.
  (4) *I wonder how it felt to be living in a great big*
        tummy.
     You'd really have to be a great big dummy.

LUCY: *(Pause)*
One day to Jonah God did speak,
For Jonah God's will seemed to seek.

LEO: *Jonah, Jonah, my son, listen to what I have to say.*
Go to Nineveh . . . to Nineveh this very day.
For those people need to call upon me and pray,
Otherwise for their wicked living they will surely
    pay.

LUCY: *But Jonah plugged his ears and his heart,*
And away from Nineveh he quickly did depart.

CHRISTOPHER: *To Nineveh . . . to Nineveh I will not go,*
Those people about God need not know.
A trip on a ship I will take,
A little vacation it will make.

LUCY: *Jonah at Joppa got on board,*
For he was running from the Lord.

WHITZIT: *The sea is as angry as it can be,*
Soon it will wash away sailors and me.
Oh, my; oh, me. What, oh, what have we done.
To bring on this storm and ruin our fun?

LUCY: *The storm grew worse and worse and worse,*
Until the captain no longer had his ship on course.

CHRISTOPHER: *The Lord I can see is after me,*
To stop the storm, toss me into the sea.

LUCY: *So into the cold, wet sea he went,*
And the Lord stopped the storm He had sent.
Jonah was swallowed by a big blue whale,
As in the water he was swimming, cold and pale.
For one day, two days, three days long,
In the whale he thought of what he'd done wrong.

CHRISTOPHER: *O Lord . . . I am sorry I disobeyed Your voice,*
It will not happen again if You give me another choice.

LUCY: *To the whale he would not be fed,*
For God spoke to Jonah, to Jonah and said:

43

LEO: *Jonah, I love you and I love the Ninevites,*
I want to help you both, days and nights.
Go now to those ones I love like you,
And to your message they will be true.

LUCY: *So God spoke once more to the great big fish,*
"Spit Jonah out on the sand near the land of
Kish."
Jonah went to Nineveh as fast as he could,
And obeyed like he knew all along he should.
(Pause.)
When God asks us something to do,
We should obey always, me and you.

HARVEY: *(Sings song again.)*
(1) *I wonder how it felt to be snatched by a great*
big mouth
As Jonah was, while running away to the South.
(2) *I wonder how it felt to be eaten in one big bite*
By a whale with a great big appetite.
(3) *I wonder how it felt to be swallowed by a great*
big whale
By a whale with a great big tail.
(4) *I wonder how it felt to be living in a great big*
tummy.
You'd really have to be a great big dummy.

CHRISTOPHER: Hope you like our poems.

LEO: Good-by. *(Growl.)*

The Calling of Peter, James, and John

SCRIPTURE: Luke 5

TRUTH: Jesus calls us to follow Him.

HARVEY: *(Holding stick with string on it and casting it as though fishing.)* Dee, dee, dum, dee, dum. There I got you! What a big fish. It must weigh 50 pounds. Oh, it's heavy. *(Lucy appears, Harvey does not see her.)* Think I'll catch another one. Come on . . . get ahold. Dee, dee, dum, dee, dee. There! Oh, this one is bigger yet. Pull, Harvey, pull. WOW! This one must weigh 85 pounds. I guess that's as many fish as I need today. *(Turns and sees Lucy.)* . . . Oh . . . hi, Lucy.

LUCY: Harvey, *what* are you doing?

HARVEY: *What* am I doing?

LUCY: What *are* you doing?

HARVEY: Why, Lucy . . . I'm fishing.

LUCY: *FISHING?*

HARVEY: Yes, fishing.

LUCY: Where's your fishing pole? Where's the water? Where are the fish? Where's the hook? Where's the bait? Oh, Harvey, do you feel OK?

HARVEY: Of course I do, Lucy. Don't you see?

LUCY: See what?

HARVEY: I was only pretending. Then I can catch any kind of fish I want. The last one I caught was a shark. He almost got me but I got him instead.

LUCY: Harvey, you are a dreamer.

WHITZIT: *(Entering)* Hi, Harvey! Hi, Lucy!

HARVEY: Hi, Whitzit.

WHITZIT: What's going on?

HARVEY: We're fishing. Want to join us?

WHITZIT: Sure, it . . .

LUCY: I am *not* fishing. Nor is Harvey.

HARVEY: I'm just pretending. Out there are lots and lots of fish to catch.

WHITZIT: Why, Lucy, we pretend fishing all the time.

LUCY: I've never heard of anything so silly.

CHRISTOPHER: *(Entering)* Looks like everyone is up bright and early today.

HARVEY: Good morning, Christopher. We're fishing. Want to join us?

CHRISTOPHER: What are you catching?

HARVEY: Last one was a shark.

CHRISTOPHER: A shark? Was it white?

HARVEY: No, it was . . .

LUCY: Christopher, they're just pretending. Harvey never caught a real shark.

CHRISTOPHER: Why, Lucy, I know that. Is there any ocean near here where we can catch a shark? When we can't really go fishing, we pretend fish. That's fun too.

LUCY: Oh, you boys!

LEO: *(Appearing)* Hello. Hello. Hello.

LUCY: Leo, at last, maybe you can help straighten out these boys. They think they are fishing. There is no water, no hooks, no fish.

LEO: Lucy, Lucy. They are pretending.

LUCY: But that's so silly.

LEO: Lucy, what were you doing yesterday afternoon?

LUCY: It was raining. I could not go outside so I stayed in my room and pretended I was a princess and . . . oh, I see now. Boys pretend other things.

46

LEO: That's right. Everyone pretends some of the time. It's fun.

HARVEY: Right!

LEO: I have an idea. Let's pretend we are living in Jesus' time. What could be happening?

CHRISTOPHER: I know. We'll be Peter, James, and John. We'll be fishing.

WHITZIT: And Jesus can call us to be His disciples.

LEO: That's good. Lucy, what can you be?

LUCY: I'll be the storyteller. You, Leo, be Jesus.

LEO: OK. Lucy, you stay over there, will you?

LUCY: I'm going.

LEO: Let's begin.
(The sound of waves.)

*LUCY: It was a beautiful morning. The sun was shining on the Sea of Galilee, making it reflect like a giant mirror. Most of the fishermen were back on shore after fishing all night. As soon as they had sold the fish they caught, they would sleep.

WHITZIT: Peter, it was sure quiet last night. I don't think a breeze blew at all.

CHRISTOPHER: There sure weren't many fish to catch either. I was hoping we would get more than this.

HARVEY: Look at this. Another net is broken. We'll have to stay up and fix it or there'll be no fishing tonight.

CHRISTOPHER: I'm already tired. . . . Say, who's that walking along the shore? The sun is so bright I can't see. He looks familiar, though.

HARVEY: It looks . . . kinda . . . like . . . Jesus. Yes . . . maybe . . . it . . . is. Yes, it *is* Jesus. Come on, let's go.
(All three exit.)

LEO: *(Appearing)* What a beautiful morning. There are Peter, James, and John. They are such good friends.

Hello. *(Yells. Whitzit, Christopher, and Harvey appear.)* I was looking for you.

CHRISTOPHER: *(Out of breath)* Good morning, Jesus. We're glad to see You.

LEO: I'm glad to see you, too. How's the fishing?

WHITZIT: Not too good. We caught only a few fish and most of our nets need mending.

HARVEY: Yes, and we are tired, too. We didn't sleep all night.

LEO: I came to talk with you about something.

HARVEY: What is it, Jesus?

LEO: First, I want us to get in your boat and move a little way from the shore. I will teach the people from the boat. *(All exit.)*

LUCY: The three men and Jesus got into the boat. Jesus taught the people who were standing on the shore. When He was finished, He had the men row out into the deep water. *(All four enter.)*

LEO: Now, men, try to catch some more fish.

CHRISTOPHER: Jesus, we fished all night and hardly caught anything. But since You told us to, we will.

LEO: Put your nets out right here.

WHITZIT: There.

HARVEY: Hey! The net is getting full.

CHRISTOPHER: It is! It is! James . . . pull! Come on, John. Pull, everyone. Pull!

WHITZIT: Look at all the fish. I have never seen so many at one time in this sea before.

CHRISTOPHER: Nor have I. Let's get them to shore.

LUCY: With their boat loaded almost to sinking with fish, the men made their way to shore.

CHRISTOPHER: I can hardly believe we caught all these fish. We won't have to work tonight.

HARVEY: Jesus, You are our Lord. We'll do anything You ask us to do.

LEO: Peter, James, John, I want you to stop fishing for fish.

WHITZIT: You mean right now?

LEO: I mean as soon as you get these fish sold. I want you to stop fishing for money forever.

CHRISTOPHER: Forever? Why, Jesus?

LEO: Because I want you to catch men for Me instead of fish. I want you to follow Me, to be My disciples and go wherever I go.

HARVEY: I want to do that.

CHRISTOPHER: But who will take care of our boats? Our nets and our jobs?

WHITZIT: Our families can. If Jesus wants us to follow Him, let's do it.

CHRISTOPHER: Yes, let's do. You are right, John. I'll follow You, Jesus.

WHITZIT: I will, too.

HARVEY: Yes. Yes, I, too, will follow You, Jesus. I want to go tell Mom and Dad about this right now. Is that OK?

LEO: Sure, John. They need to know.

CHRISTOPHER: When do we begin?

LEO: Tonight we leave for Jerusalem.

WHITZIT: We will be ready. *(All exit.)*

LUCY: From that day on, Peter, James, and John became Jesus' disciples. They followed Jesus wherever He went. They were no longer fishers of fish but fishers of men. As Jesus called these men to follow Him, He wants us to follow Him, too. Will you let Jesus lead your life? Will you follow Him? I hope you will. Goodby.

Philip and the Ethiopian

SCRIPTURE: Acts 8:26-40

CONCEPT: God uses many ways to tell others about Jesus.

HARVEY: Rmm. Rmm. Rmm. *(Sound of a car motor racing. Harvey is holding a steering wheel, Whitzit watches.)* Hold on, here we go. Rmm. Rmm. Rmm.

WHITZIT: Harvey, this is fun. Can I drive for a while?

HARVEY: Rmm. Rmm. Rmm. Sure, Whitzit. Here . . . *(passes steering wheel to Whitzit.)*

WHITZIT: Rmm. Rmm. Rmm. Urrch. Here we come to another curve. Urrrch.

HARVEY: There's Lucy. Stop and let's pick her up.

WHITZIT: Urrrrrrrrch.

HARVEY: Lucy, you want a ride?

LUCY: What?

HARVEY: Do you want a ride in our super deluxe sport convertible? Whitzit is driving.

LUCY: Sure, Harvey.

HARVEY: Get in. *(She gets in as though entering back seat of car.)*

WHITZIT: Rmm. Rmm. Rmm. Urrrch. Rmm. Rmm. Rmm.

LUCY: What fun! I love to ride in a red convertible.

HARVEY: Lucy, the car is blue.

LUCY: Oh, so it is. What a lovely shade of blue!

WHITZIT: Rmm. Rmm. Rmm. Here comes another curve. *(All three lean.)* Urrrrrrch. Urrrrrch.

LUCY: Whitzit, slow down.

WHITZIT: Why, Lucy?

LUCY: There's Christopher up ahead. Let's pick him up.

WHITZIT: OK.

HARVEY: And I get to drive now.

WHITZIT: OK. Urrrrch.

LUCY: Christopher, oh, Christopher! Come ride with us.

CHRISTOPHER: *(Off stage.)* What's going on?

LUCY: We're going for a ride in this red convertible.

HARVEY: Lucy! It's blue, not red!

LUCY: Right! Christopher, we are going for a ride in this super blue convertible. Come join us.

CHRISTOPHER: OK, I will. *(Gets in beside Lucy.)*

HARVEY: Here we go. Rmm. Rmm. Rmm. Urrrrch. Urrrrch. Rmm. Rmm. Rmm.

CHRISTOPHER: Wow. Harvey is a good driver. When did you learn to drive?

HARVEY: Oh, I just practiced and practiced until I knew how.

LUCY: I think we'd better get home. Leo will be hunting for us soon.

HARVEY: OK. Home, here we come. Rmm. Rmm. Rmm. Urrrrch. Urrrrch. Rmm. Rmm.

WHITZIT: . . . And here we are. Everyone out. *(All out and exit.) (Leo enters.)*

LEO: Where are those kids? Lucy! Harvey! Christopher! Whitzit! *(All enter.)*

CHRISTOPHER: Did you call, Leo?

LEO: Yes, where have you been?

LUCY: We went for a ride with Harvey in his red convertible.

HARVEY: Lucy, it's *blue.*

LUCY: Oh, yes. We went for a ride in Harvey's blue convertible. Was it ever fun!

WHITZIT: I wonder what kind of car Jesus drove.

LEO: Oh, Whitzit. Jesus did not drive a car. There were no cars when He lived on the earth.

LUCY: How did He travel?

LEO: He walked everywhere He went, or He rode a donkey.

CHRISTOPHER: Did anyone ride in anything?

LEO: Yes, the Bible tells about a man who lived in Ethiopia who worked for a king and queen. He had a chariot. A chariot is a kind of cart pulled by horses. One year he drove all the way to Jerusalem for a religious celebration. On the way home he was reading the Bible. A man came running up to the chariot as it drove along. His name was Philip. Philip asked the man what he was reading. The Ethiopian said he was reading from the prophet Isaiah.

LUCY: I remember the story, Leo. Can we act it out?

LEO: Sure, Lucy. Let's see. Whitzit, you drive. Harvey, you be Philip, and Christopher, you be the Ethiopian. Lucy, you tell the story. *(All exit but Lucy.)*

LUCY: It was a beautiful spring morning. The road was quiet as the man from Ethiopia rode along. *(Whitzit and Christopher appear.)* He was reading a scroll.

CHRISTOPHER: "He was led as a sheep to the slaughter; and like a lamb dumb before his shearer, so opened he not his mouth. . . ." Say what is that running toward us?

WHITZIT: It's a man. Looks like he wants to talk to us.

CHRISTOPHER: Stop the chariot. Let's see what he wants. *(Pause.)* Hello there! Climb in if you're going our way.

HARVEY: Thanks. *(puff, puff)* I see you have a scroll. What are you reading?

CHRISTOPHER: I'm reading from the prophet Isaiah.

HARVEY: Do you know what you are reading about?

CHRISTOPHER: No, I don't. Can you tell me?

HARVEY: Yes, I think I can.

CHRISTOPHER: Who's the fellow writing about?

LUCY: As the two rode along, Philip told the Ethiopian that the scroll he was reading taught about Jesus; that Jesus would come to earth and suffer and die that he might be forgiven of his sins, and that He would be his friend and help him every day. All he had to do was ask Jesus to come into his heart as his Lord and Master.

CHRISTOPHER: Is there any reason why I cannot become a Christian?

HARVEY: Do you believe Jesus is the Son of God?

CHRISTOPHER: Yes, I do.

HARVEY: Do you believe He can forgive your sins?

CHRISTOPHER: Yes, I know He can.

HARVEY: Will you ask Him to forgive you and come into your heart?

CHRISTOPHER: I already have. And He has come into my heart.

HARVEY: That makes you a Christian.

CHRISTOPHER: I want to be baptized right away, too.

HARVEY: That's a good idea.

CHRISTOPHER: Driver, there's water ahead. Stop so Philip can baptize me. I want the world to know I'm a Christian. *(All exit but Lucy.)*

LUCY: That is how the Ethiopian became a Christian. Right in his chariot with Philip. *(Exits as Leo enters.)*

LEO: Boys and girls, have you become Christians, too, like the Ethiopian did? I hope so. Good-by. *(Growl.)*

The Healing of the Lame Man

SCRIPTURE: Luke 5:17-26

CONCEPT: God helps us to do things for Him.

HARVEY: Doo, dee doo, etc. *(Offstage and then appearing, looks around and does a slow "doo, dee dum" in time to his turning head.)* Hey! What happened? Where am I? Who are all of you people? What's that bright light shining in my eyes? Lucy! Lucy!

LUCY: Harvey, what on earth is wrong?

HARVEY: Lucy! Lucy!

LUCY: Harvey . . . *(Touches him.)* I'm right here.

HARVEY: *(Puts on sunglasses.)* Oh, I couldn't see you. Those dumb bright lights are hurting my eyes and blinding me.

LUCY: Well, I like them. *(Straightens her hair and clothes.)* I like to be up front with everyone looking at me.

HARVEY: I don't. What are all those people doing staring at me?

LUCY: Harvey, have you forgotten?

HARVEY: Forgotten what?

LUCY: That today we tell these people the story of Jesus healing the lame man?

HARVEY: Yeh.

LUCY: Yeh, what?

HARVEY: Yeh, I forgot.

LUCY: You'd better hurry. It's time to start. *(Both exit, Leo appears at the side like a narrator.)*

LEO: One warm day in July, two brothers were talking.

HARVEY: Say, Christopher, did you hear our neighbor Levi last night?

CHRISTOPHER: I sure did, Harvey. He was crying all night. Do you suppose he was in that much pain?

HARVEY: I think he was. I wish there would be someone or someway to help him.

CHRISTOPHER: Me, too. *(Lucy appears.)* Hi, Lucy. Why are you out of breath?

LUCY: Harvey! Christopher! I just saw Jesus go into Benjamin's house with a lot of important people.

HARVEY: Jesus? What's He doing in town?

LUCY: I don't know. But I thought maybe . . . well . . . you see . . . I thought . . .

CHRISTOPHER: You thought what, Lucy?

LUCY: It's Levi.

HARVEY: Levi?

LUCY: Yes, Levi. If we could get him to Jesus, Jesus might heal him. Levi kept me awake half the night with his crying.

HARVEY: Me, too. But do you think Jesus could heal him?

CHRISTOPHER: Of course He could. But how will we get Levi to Jesus? Levi can't walk. *(Whitzit appears.)*

WHITZIT: What's going on?

LUCY: Jesus is at Benjamin's house and we want to take Levi to Him. But how can we?

WHITZIT: We can carry him. I know where a stretcher is.

HARVEY: That's a good idea. Go get it, will you?

WHITZIT: Sure. *(Exits.)*

CHRISTOPHER: Together, we can carry Levi to Jesus. *(They all exit.)*

55

LEO: The four of them took the stretcher and went to Levi's house. There they told him they wanted to take him to Jesus so Jesus could heal him. *(Pause)* He agreed and the four of them carried him to Jesus. They arrived at Benjamin's house and set Levi down for a rest. *(The four appear.)*

HARVEY: Lucy, you sure are doing a good job.

LUCY: Thanks, Harvey. Whitzit, could you go ahead and clear a way into the house? There are a lot of people in the way.

WHITZIT: Sure thing. *(He exits, while the other three look to one side as though they are watching Whitzit.)*

CHRISTOPHER: Look, the people are pushing Whitzit down. He's trying to get up.

LUCY: Oh *(covering her eyes)*. I can't look.

HARVEY: He got up. He's trying again. No! Someone tried to hit him. Here he comes back.

WHITZIT: I can't get through.

CHRISTOPHER: What can we do?

HARVEY: I've got an idea. Let's get him on the roof. It's flat. We can open up a hole by removing some tiles and let him down by ropes to Jesus.

LUCY: But who will pay for the damage?

HARVEY: I have 3 dollars and 27 cents.

WHITZIT: I have 4 dollars and 12 cents.

CHRISTOPHER: I have 18 dollars and 66 cents.

LUCY: I have 47 dollars. That makes *(pause)* let's see *(pause)* 70 *(pause)* 3 dollars and *(pause)* 5 cents. That will pay for the roof. Let's go! *(They all exit.)*

LEO: So the four of them carried Levi up the side stairs to the roof of the house where they tore a hole in it and let Levi down into the room where Jesus was sitting. *(Four appear, all looking down.)*

LUCY: Look! Jesus sees him!

HARVEY: So do the rich guys.

CHRISTOPHER: Jesus is talking to Levi. He's telling him his sins are forgiven.

WHITZIT: Levi is crying he's so happy.

HARVEY: What is Jesus saying now?

CHRISTOPHER: *(As though repeating.)* Get up. Pick up your stretcher and walk out of here.

LUCY: Look! *(Very excited.)* Look! Look! Levi is moving!

WHITZIT: He's getting up!

CHRISTOPHER: He's walking!

HARVEY: Levi has been healed by Jesus.

ALL FOUR: Hooray! Hooray! *(All exit.)*

LEO: Levi was healed. The roof was repaired. And Levi's four friends, along with Levi, loved and served Jesus the rest of their lives. *(Pause.)* That's just like Jesus, to do nice things for those in need. And isn't it good to have friends who help others get to Jesus! Jesus is wonderful. Wonderful. Wonderful! *(Growl and exit.)*

✳   ✳   ✳

The Story of the Tree Climber

SCRIPTURE: Luke 19:1-10

CONCEPT: When Jesus comes into our lives, He changes them.

LUCY: Hello. Hello. Hello. I want to tell you about a tree climber.

HARVEY: Pardon me, sister, but did I hear you say a tree climber?

LUCY: Yes, Harvey, a tree climber.

HARVEY: I've heard of a mountain climber but I thought it was just kids who climbed trees.

LUCY: Not this time.

HARVEY: Well, hurry up and tell us.

LUCY: The place where the tree climber lived was Jericho, a city down by the Jordan River below Jerusalem. This tree climber had big, strong muscles.

HARVEY: Kinda like mine?

LUCY: Oh . . . do you have muscles?

HARVEY: Sister, just for that you get to feel them. *(He hits Lucy.)*

LUCY: Ouch! Harvey, you hurt me! Ooooooooh.

CHRISTOPHER: Is it possible for anyone around here to get a little peace and quiet in which to study? What is happening, anyway?

HARVEY: I have been unjustly insulted.

LUCY: I have been unjustly slugged.

CHRISTOPHER: What is it, anyway?

LUCY: Really, we got talking about muscles when we were talking about the tree climber. I was telling about him and got rudely interrupted. May I continue? *(Both nod their heads yes.)* As I was saying, this man had big muscles. But he was short. Very short. He did not like to miss important things and often used his big muscles to get his little body to the front of a crowd.

One day he heard that a great Man named Jesus was coming to town. He wanted to see Jesus. But the crowd was too big and he was too short to see the road. Like always, he tried pushing his way to the front, using his muscles. About halfway to the front, he elbowed a big man who had bigger muscles. Before he knew what had happened, he was sitting on the ground at the back of the crowd.

HARVEY: Lucy, did the little guy give up?

LUCY: No, he did not. He got a great idea. He saw a tree down the road. It was a sycamore tree with limbs that hung over the road. With his strong muscles he climbed it and sat where he could easily see Jesus when He came along.

WHITZIT: *(Appearing and laughing.)*

LUCY: Whitzit, why are you laughing?

WHITZIT: Because I think it's funny.

CHRISTOPHER: What's so funny?

WHITZIT: A grown man sitting in a tree. I'll bet everyone was laughing at him.

CHRISTOPHER: What happened next?

LUCY: Jesus came by and saw that little man sitting in the tree. He told him to come down. Jesus wanted to go to his house. The tree climber jumped down and the two walked home together. At the house, the little man told Jesus he loved Him and would do whatever Jesus wanted him to do. Jesus told him to do his best to fix up all the wrong things he had done.

HARVEY: Did he do it?

LUCY: Yes, he did. The ones he had cheated he paid what he owed them. Those he had lied to, he told them he was sorry.

WHITZIT: That would be hard to do.

CHRISTOPHER: Yes, it would. But it would be worth it. You know something? I think this man was the happiest that day he had ever been in his life.

WHITZIT, LUCY, and HARVEY: So do I. *(Exit.)*

LEO: *(Appearing)* I listened to Lucy's story. It is fun to hear about people who meet Jesus and love and serve Him. I want Harvey to come back and sing the song about that little man tree climber, Zacchaeus. Sing with him if you know it. (Harvey reappears.)

SONG: *Zacchaeus was a wee little man, a wee little man was he.*
He climbed up into a sycamore tree, for the Lord he wanted to see.
And as the Saviour passed that way, He looked up in the tree.
And He said, "Zacchaeus, you come down, for I'm going to your house today, for I'm going to your house today."†

LEO: Are you Jesus' friend? I am. Will you do what He wants you to do? I hope so. Good-by. *(Growl.)*

---

†In *Action No. 1* (Singspiration Music)

Palm Sunday

SCRIPTURE: Matthew 21
TRUTH: Christ is King

HARVEY: Hosanna! Hosanna! Hosanna! *(Waving a dead tree branch.)*
LUCY: Harvey.
HARVEY: Hosanna! Hosanna! Hosanna!
LUCY: Harvey!

HARVEY: Oh, hi, Lucy. Hosanna! Hosanna! Hosanna!

LUCY: Harvey! Will you stop that and tell me what you are doing?

HARVEY: Lucy, I was just reading about Jesus riding into Jerusalem years ago on a donkey.

LUCY: What does a donkey have to do with what you're doing?

HARVEY: The Bible tells that all the people waved branches and shouted Hosanna! Hosanna! Hosanna! as He rode into town.

LUCY: You yell so loud it hurts my ears. And that branch would hurt the donkey. I'm afraid you would have scared everyone if you were there.

HARVEY: Lucy, I find it hard to believe my happy hosanna! hosanna! hosanna! would frighten anyone.

LUCY: It does me!

WHITZIT: Hey, what goes on here? Harvey, don't hit Lucy with that stick. Those noises are scaring everyone. Please be more careful.

LUCY: See, I told you!

HARVEY: Whitzit, I was all alone reliving Palm Sunday when Lucy interrupted me.

WHITZIT: Palm Sunday? Where's your palm?

HARVEY: Here. *(Holds up stick.)*

WHITZIT: That?

HARVEY: Well, I guess it doesn't exactly look like a palm leaf. I pretended it was.

LUCY: See, I told you!

CHRISTOPHER: I heard some terrible sounds up here. What were they?

LUCY: Harvey was pretending he was in the Palm Sunday parade when Jesus rode into Jerusalem. That stick was his palm leaf.

CHRISTOPHER: Oh, no! How funny! Harvey, you are something else. I suppose those loud yells were your Hosannas. *(Christopher, Lucy, Whitzit laugh.)*

LEO: *(Growling)* I don't like the sounds I have been hearing. What is happening?

CHRISTOPHER: Oh, Leo, you were hearing Harvey pretending he was in the Palm Sunday parade. He was so funny. He used an old stick for a palm leaf and was saying Hosanna in the worst voice.

LUCY: He was really funny. *(All three laugh.)*

LEO: *(Growl.)* Just a minute. What I heard was not Harvey but you, Lucy; and you, Whitzit; and you, Christopher.

WHITZIT: Us? Why, Harvey was the one causing all the trouble.

CHRISTOPHER: And making all the silly sounds.

LUCY: And waving that old stick.

LEO: How were *you* three celebrating Palm Sunday? Have you read or even thought about the story? *(They shake their heads no.)* At least Harvey was thinking about it. And you were making fun of him. Your making fun was much worse than what he did.

CHRISTOPHER: You're right, Leo. Harvey, we are sorry.

WHITZIT: Yes, we are.

LUCY: Could you tell us the story, Harvey?

HARVEY: Sure, gang. Jesus and His disciples were coming to the city of Jerusalem after a long walk in the hot sun. Jesus told some of His disciples to go to a friend's house and borrow a donkey for Him to ride.

LUCY: I remember what happened. The disciples went for the donkey and brought it back along with a colt. Jesus climbed on the donkey and rode it into Jerusalem.

HARVEY: That's right, Lucy. As He was riding toward town, the disciples laid their clothes on the ground for the donkey to walk over. A lot of others saw what was happening and ran to join in the celebration. They formed a parade. Nearby were palm trees. Some of the people took palm leaves and began waving them. Others laid them on the roadway.

CHRISTOPHER: But what about the Hosannas?

HARVEY: All the people in the parade wanted to know who Jesus was. They found out He was Jesus of Nazareth who said He was their new king, king of their hearts. When people realized how important He was they waved their palm branches and began singing out . . .

LEO: We know, Harvey. They said "Hosanna. Blessed is our King!"

HARVEY: And they waved palm branches. *(Harvey waves his stick, almost hitting Lucy who ducks.)*

LUCY: Here, let me wave it. *(She takes the stick.)*

HARVEY: Everyone celebrated because Jesus, God's Son, came to earth. He is my Friend and Savior, too, so I like to celebrate Palm Sunday.

CHRISTOPHER: That's today!

LEO: And, my friends, it is more important what is in your heart than how good your voice sounds or how fancy a branch you wave.

LUCY: Let's all say it. Hosanna! Hosanna! Hosanna!

HARVEY: I'm glad we're all celebrating Palm Sunday. Hosanna! Hosanna! Hosanna! *(All exit.)*

Easter

CONCEPT: What is inside the heart is more important than the clothes we wear.

LUCY: Harvey. Harvey. Harvey! Come here. Come here!

HARVEY: Lucy. Lucy. Lucy! Here I am. Here I am!

LUCY: Will you stop it?

HARVEY: No. No. No!

LUCY: OK, then just leave.

HARVEY: No. No. No! Why did you call me?

LUCY: I wanted to tell you about my new Easter dress. It's yellow with cute little flowers all over it, lace at the neck and arms, and a big ribbon in back.

HARVEY: That's so exciting I think I'll go get one just like it. *(Laughs.)*

LUCY: Harvey!

CHRISTOPHER: *(Appearing to the side.)* Well, I see Lucy and Harvey are at it again. They seem to find more reasons to fight than they do reasons to get along. *(To Harvey and Lucy.)* Good morning! You both look happy.

LUCY: We are. We are.

HARVEY: We are? We are?

LUCY: I was just telling Harvey about my new Easter dress with its flowers and lace and ribbon.

CHRISTOPHER: I saw it, Lucy.

LUCY: You did? When?

CHRISTOPHER: At the store. A lady was buying it.

LUCY: No. Oh, no! Ooohhhhh.

HARVEY: No? Oh, no? Ooohhhhh? But I thought you already had the dress.

LUCY: No. I was going to get it today. I finally had enough money to pay for it.

HARVEY: Are you sure someone bought it, Christopher?

CHRISTOPHER: Yes, I am sure. I was in the Fashion Bar looking for some new clothes and saw Lucy try it on.

LUCY: And it was the only one like it. Oh. Oooohhh.

HARVEY: It was the only one like it? Oh? Oooohhh? Lucy, can't you get another dress?

LUCY: Ohhh. Ohhh. Ohhh. *(All exit, Leo and Whitzit appear.)*

WHITZIT: Leo, why is Lucy crying?

LEO: Because the new Easter dress she wanted is sold.

WHITZIT: But why is she crying?

LEO: New dresses are important to girls. Especially at Easter.

WHITZIT: Why, Leo?

LEO: It must be because they like to look fresh and dress in new things.

WHITZIT: Why at Easter time?

LEO: At Easter time we celebrate the new life we have in Jesus.

WHITZIT: Yes, Jesus does give us new life. Leo, is it more important to have new outsides like clothes or a new inside because Jesus is in your heart?

LEO: New outside clothes cannot change the inside. Only Jesus can do that. If you are new inside, the clothes outside are not so important.

WHITZIT: I'm going to go tell Lucy. *(Exits.)*

65

LEO: That's true, boys and girls. If Jesus is in your heart, it doesn't matter how new or old your clothes are. Aren't you glad Jesus can make you feel good inside? Even if your clothes are not new? I'd better go talk with Lucy, too. Lucy. Lucy! *(Growl. Exit.)*

✳ ✳ ✳

Easter

CONCEPT: Jesus is alive and with us right now.

LEO: Say, boys and girls. I always like to hear the Easter story. It is fun to hear over and over.

CHRISTOPHER: I've been thinking about what it must have been like to have been there that day Jesus arose from the grave.

LUCY: How do you think you would have felt, Christopher?

CHRISTOPHER: I'm not sure. Maybe a little shocked. A lot surprised.

LUCY: How about you, Whitzit?

WHITZIT: I don't know. It would be too wonderful to think about.

LUCY: Harvey, have you thought how you would have felt?

HARVEY: I sure have. I would have been scared. Those angels would have looked like ghosts. I don't think I would have wanted to stay around long. I think I would have run.

LEO: The Bible tells us everyone was scared. Some ran away, others fainted. The angels told them not to be afraid. *(Pause.)* If you were not afraid, how would you feel?

LUCY: I would be happy. Very happy.

LEO: Why, Lucy?

LUCY: Because Jesus could be with me all the time—when I was afraid, when I was happy or sad—all the time.

CHRISTOPHER: You know something?

WHITZIT: What, Christopher?

CHRISTOPHER: Jesus was not only alive *then*, he is alive *now*.

HARVEY: And He is with us right now. In this room.

LEO: That's right. The Easter story is not like a fairy tale. It is true. And it tells us what Jesus is like today.

HARVEY: Jesus wants to help us.

CHRISTOPHER: He wants to teach us.

LUCY: He also wants to be our Friend.

WHITZIT: And be with us all the time.

LUCY: I was wondering about one thing, though.

HARVEY: What was that, Lucy?

LUCY: How can He do all these things for us?

HARVEY: I think we just have to ask Him to do them. Is that right, Leo?

LEO: Yes, that's true. Jesus will be with us. He'll help us. He'll teach us the right things to do. He'll be our Friend *if* we ask Him.

CHRISTOPHER: I'd like to ask Him to help me and be with me.

HARVEY: Me, too. Say, what about you boys and girls out there? Do you want to ask Jesus to help you? To be with you? To be your Friend? He will, you know.

67

Raise your hand if you want to pray with me. *(Pause.)* Good. Now let's pray. Pray what I say quietly to yourself. *(Pause after each phrase.)* Jesus, I know You are alive. I know You are with us today. Will You please be with me all the time? Will You be my special Friend? Will You help me when I need You? Will You teach me to do good? Thank You. I love You. Amen.

LEO: We are all glad Jesus is alive. Happy Easter. And Happy Every Day!

* * *

The Easter Story

(A Sunday School Program)

CHRISTOPHER: Now, Harvey and Whitzit, today we cannot mess up. Everyone will be here to hear the Easter story and we must do a good job. Do you hear that? A good job!

WHITZIT: Yes. A good job.

HARVEY: A super-duper job. Christopher, old buddy, I'll do a deluxe job!

CHRISTOPHER: I sure hope so. We simply can't have you and Lucy arguing.

HARVEY: I'll try.

LUCY: *(Sneaking up on Harvey)* Booooo!

HARVEY: Yikes!

LUCY: At last! At last! I scared you instead of you scaring me. Oh, I've wanted to do that for a long time.

HARVEY: Oh!

LUCY: Harvey, are you sick? I scared you and surprised you and all you can say is "oh"? Why aren't you yelling and fighting back? Afraid of your sister?

HARVEY: No.

LUCY: I think you are. Scaredy-cat! Scaredy-cat!

CHRISTOPHER: Lucy! I had just asked Harvey not to fight with you and here you are causing all sorts of commotion. This is Easter Sunday. We want to do our best.

LUCY: Oh, he's not sick then. Too bad.

WHITZIT: Anyway, both of us said we would cooperate. Will you?

LUCY: I always am good. It's you and Harvey who cause all the trouble and . . .

CHRISTOPHER: Lucy! Will you help?

LUCY: All right. Since this is Easter.

LEO: I see you are all ready to present the Easter story. And you're quiet. Good. Shall we begin? *(Stop tape.)*
"Comes the Wondrous Hour"†—Children's Choir

LUCY: Jesus had been born in Bethlehem of Judea about 33 years before. He had grown up in Nazareth and so was called a Nazarene. He was a carpenter, a teacher, and a preacher.

CHRISTOPHER: After teaching the multitudes and His 12 disciples for about three years, His enemies began to plan how to kill Him. Even one of the 12 disciples, Judas Iscariot, helped the enemies catch Him.

HARVEY: One Sunday, Jesus rode into Jerusalem on a donkey. Lots of people formed a parade, shouting, "Hosanna! Blessed is He who comes!" They waved palm branches and placed coats in the path. More and more people joined the celebration. *(Stop tape.)*
"Hosanna Be the Children's Song"†—Kindergarten

†In *Children's Praises* (Lillenas Publishing Co.)

children walk around the sanctuary waving palm branches while some child sings.

WHITZIT: On Thursday evening, Jesus gathered His disciples in the Upper Room where He told them He was about to die. He served them bread and said it represented His broken body. Then He served them grape juice and said it represented His blood. Christians all over the world remember His death by taking two things in Communion. *(Stop tape.)*

"Let Us Break Bread Together on Our Knees"‡—Solo by a child

LEO: On Friday, there was a trial and Jesus was pronounced guilty for saying He was God. They said He would have to die. After being beaten, He was forced to carry a cross through town and then was nailed to it. There just outside the city gate, He died. *(Stop tape.)*

*"Were You There?"** (first verse) Trio of children. *(Group of girls in costume go to cross and stand.)*

LUCY: Jesus was buried late Friday afternoon. A seal was set on the tomb so no one could open it. Guards were kept outside it all the time. *(Stop tape.)*

"Were You There?" (second verse)—Trio of children. *(Girls go to tomb and wait in darkness.)*

WHITZIT: Saturday, nothing happened.

LEO: Early on Sunday morning some women went to the tomb to be sure everything was OK. It was just beginning to get light. When they arrived at the tomb, they found it opened and a bright light shone from it. *(Stop tape.) (Lights on. Girls see angels—nursery class with tinsel ring on their heads surround the tomb.)*

‡In *Reasons to Sing* (Lillenas Publishing Co.)
*In *Chorus Choir Voices No. 1* (Lillenas Publishing Co.)

HARVEY: An angel spoke to them and said, "Jesus is not here. He has risen as He said He would." Jesus arose and He is alive today. *(Stop tape.)*

"Christ the Lord Is Risen Today"†—Children's Choir

CHRISTOPHER: Today we celebrate that day Jesus arose. But really we can celebrate every day, because Jesus is alive all the time and can be in all our hearts. *(Stop tape.)*

"Comes the Wondrous Hour"—Children's Choir

LUCY: I sure love the Easter story.

CHRISTOPHER: I do, too. It helps me remember God is greater than any problems.

WHITZIT: Me too.

HARVEY: I'm glad Jesus is alive and with us right now.

LEO: And that's what Easter is all about. Jesus is alive! I hope all of you have Easter every day. Happy Easter! Happy Every Day! *(All wave and exit.)*

✳ ✳ ✳

Christmas

CONCEPT: Christmas is more than material gifts.

HARVEY: *(Holding a long piece of paper.)* Dee, dee, dum, dum, dum. Let's see. I think I have everything on my list. A football, an electric train, a 25-pound box of Sweet Tarts, model cars of the 1947 Chevy, the 1962 Ford, the . . .

LUCY: Harvey. What in the world are you doing with that long, long piece of paper?

†In *Children's Praises* (Lillenas Publishing Co.)

71

HARVEY: It's the final draft of all the things I want for Christmas.

LUCY: You sure want a lot of things.

HARVEY: I guess I do, don't I?

LUCY: You sure do. I personally want just a few items. My list is hardly big enough to fill my hand.

HARVEY: Can I see your list?

LUCY: You most certainly cannot!

HARVEY: *(Grabs list from her.)* Don't be so sneaky. Let's see. A 1976 Mercedes pulling a 15-foot trailer, a six month's vacation in Paris, a private ski resort . . .

LUCY: Give me my list!

HARVEY: No wonder your list is so small. One of your things costs more than all of my things put together.

LUCY: Give me my list! *(Begins fighting with him.)*

LEO: *(Growl.)* My children, what is going on?

HARVEY: I just was looking at her list of things she wants for Christmas.

LEO: List? Of things she *wants?* I do not understand. I thought Christmas was a time of *giving.* Where are your lists of things you intend to *give?*

LUCY: I don't have any list like that.

HARVEY: I don't have any either.

LEO: My children, you must make a list like that. Christmas is a time of sharing. If you do not share, then you will not have a good Christmas.

HARVEY and LUCY: Thanks, Leo. We'll go make one. *(Exit.)*

LEO: *(Christopher and Whitzit enter.)* Do you have your lists ready?

CHRISTOPHER: Here is mine. I plan to give Lucy a ribbon for her hair. A new button to Harvey that says, "Jesus Is the Hope." And . . .

LEO: That is not exactly what I had in mind. I wanted you to make a list of things you could give or do for someone who could not give or do back for you.

WHITZIT: I have my list. I am going to give a toy truck to the boy who lives down the block from us. He is friendly to us.

CHRISTOPHER: I'm going to hang up my clothes every night. And make my bed every morning without someone telling me.

LEO: That is a good present. *(Whitzit and Christopher exit. Harvey and Lucy enter.)*

HARVEY: Leo, here is my new list.

LEO: Let's see. It says, "I'm going to give everyone a smile even when I don't feel like it." Good, Harvey! Now, Lucy?

LUCY: My present to everyone is an ear.

HARVEY: An ear? I don't want any ear!

LUCY: What I mean is, I am going to listen more. *And not talk so much.*

LEO: That is the kind of lists I like. I know you will all have a Merry Christmas this year. *(Whitzit and Christopher appear.)*

ALL: *Merry Christmas, boys and girls . . . Merry Christmas!*

Caring

CONCEPT: Prayer helps in time of need.

LEO: *(Growl.)* Hi, boys and girls! How is everyone? I have some good news for you. Whitzit has been sick with the flu all week. Oh, no, that's not the good news. The good news is that Whitzit is better now. He *was* sick. Now he's well. Isn't that good news?

LUCY: *(Coughs two or three times offstage before appearing. Keeps hand over mouth a lot.)* Leo, there you are. I have been *(cough, cough)* looking all over for you *(cough, cough)*.

LEO: Sounds like you should be in bed, not out here with all these boys and girls.

LUCY: I'm keeping my hand *(cough, cough)* over my mouth. But I must talk to you. It is very *(cough, cough)* important.

LEO: OK, Lucy, what do you want?

LUCY: You see *(cough, cough)* it's Harvey. He has been gone all day and I'm worried about him.

LEO: Really? Are you sure he didn't just go shopping or visiting a friend?

LUCY: No, Leo *(cough, cough)*, he got up real early this morning, got dressed, and left quietly. He thought I was asleep *(cough, cough, cough)* but I saw him leave.

LEO: Maybe the others know where he is. Christopher! Whitzit! *(Lucy coughs. They appear.)*

74

WHITZIT: Did you want us?

LEO: Yes. We have a problem. *(Lucy coughs.)*

WHITZIT: We see her!

LUCY: I am not the problem. *(Cough, cough.)*

WHITZIT: You sound like it!

LUCY: Leo . . . *(cough, cough)* . . . make him stop.

LEO: *(Growl.)*

WHITZIT: Sorry, sis. *(Lucy coughs.)*

CHRISTOPHER: If Lucy is not our difficulty, and she surely does sound like it, then what must it be? It is indeed serious. I assure you all my power of arm, or brain, or time is at your disposal to solve this difficult dilemma.

LEO: Thanks, Christopher. How about you, Whitzit? *(Lucy coughs.)*

WHITZIT: What about me?

LEO: Will you help us?

WHITZIT: Sure.

LEO: Good. We'll begin right now.

CHRISTOPHER: Leo . . .

LEO: Yes, Christopher?

CHRISTOPHER: You haven't told us the problem yet.

LEO: So I haven't. *(Lucy coughs.)* The problem is Harvey. He's gone. Missing. No one knows where he is. *(Christopher and Whitzit look all over.)*

WHITZIT: I can't see him.

CHRISTOPHER: Me neither. *(Lucy coughs.)*

LEO: But we must find him.

WHITZIT: I'll call the police. *(Disappears fast.)*

LEO: Whitzit . . . too late.

LUCY: I'll call the fire department. *(Disappears fast.)*

LEO: Lucy . . . too late for her, too.

CHRISTOPHER: I'll go look for him. *(Disappears.)*

LEO: Maybe I had better wait here. *(Looks around.)* I have an idea. While they are looking, I'll pray. *(Bows head.)* Jesus, help us find Harvey safe. Amen. *(Looks around, quietly . . . then he hears whistling far off, gets louder, then Harvey appears.)* Harvey! Harvey! It's so good to see you. Oooohhhh.

HARVEY: Leo, it's good to see you, too.

LEO: Christopher, Lucy, Whitzit! Christopher, Lucy, Whitzit! Christopher, Lucy, Whitzit! *(They appear and see Harvey, hug him.)*

LUCY: Harvey, my sweet brother! How good to see you. *(Cough, cough.)*

HARVEY: Hi, sis!

CHRISTOPHER: How good to have you home again, Harvey.

HARVEY: Home? Again? Was I gone?

WHITZIT: Harvey, we love you and we missed you.

HARVEY: Missed me? How could you miss me?

LUCY: Why, Harvey. You've been gone all morning and we have been worried about you. I called the fire department.

WHITZIT: And I called the police.

HARVEY: The police?

CHRISTOPHER: And I went hunting for you.

HARVEY: For me?

LEO: And I prayed for you. *(Quiet.)*

WHITZIT, CHRISTOPHER, LUCY: You prayed?

LUCY: I never thought of that!

WHITZIT: Me neither.

HARVEY: Thank you all for caring. And that you, Leo, remembered to pray for me. I needed it. During the night Lucy coughed so much I decided to get her some cough drops as soon as the drugstore opened. But on the way home I was almost hit by a car. If you had not prayed, I might have been hurt. Thank you. And Lucy, I hope the cough drops help your cough.

LUCY: Thanks, Harvey. Let's all go get them.

LEO: Don't forget, Lucy, when you have troubles. It is wise to pray.

LUCY: *(Cough, cough.)* OK, Leo, I'll remember. *(All exit.)*

✳ ✳ ✳

Missionary Offering

CONCEPT: Not everyone can know about Jesus through use of the English language; we must reach people with their own.

CHRISTOPHER: *Buenos dias, Amigos.*

WHITZIT: Huh?

CHRISTOPHER: *Buenos dias, Amigos.*

WHITZIT: Lucy! Lucy!

LUCY: (Appearing) Whitzit, what's wrong?

WHITZIT: Christopher is sick!

CHRISTOPHER: I am not sick.

WHITZIT: You sure sounded like it.

CHRISTOPHER: All I was doing was greeting our good friends out there in Spanish.

LUCY: Oh, that's right. Today is the day we take our offering to help tell the gospel in Spanish, Portuguese, French, Italian, Danish, German, and other languages.

WHITZIT: Why do we have to tell the gospel in any language besides English? I can't understand those other languages.

CHRISTOPHER: Other people cannot understand English. If we are going to tell them about Jesus, it must be in their own language. Spanish for those who speak Spanish. French for those who speak French. German for those who speak German.

LUCY: I thought I might ask the missionaries to let me go to a Spanish country.

WHITZIT: You?

LUCY: Yes, me. I would sing. Listen. *(Sings a Spanish song.)*

CHRISTOPHER: How about taking the offering instead of singing?

LUCY: Harvey is supposed to do that. *(All exit. Harvey comes in.)*

HARVEY: Today it is *my* privilege to give *you* the privilege of helping tell thousands of people about Jesus, people whose language you do not speak. Will you give a few extra dollars to help? I believe we have ushers to lift the offering. Yes, and we have someone to play music for us, too. Let's pray. Then you give your dollars. "God, we thank You for having someone tell us about Jesus in our language. We want others to hear about Him in their own language. Bless our gifts to that end. Amen."